This book belongs to
_____

___   ___

A little note from the author...

Dua means to make a prayer.
Allah is the Arabic word for God.
Allahu Akbar means Allah is Almighty.

For Ibrahim & Hannah

First published in Great Britain in 2009, revised edition
published 2011 by Greenbird Books
©2011 Anaya Nayeer
The right of Anaya Nayeer to be identified as
Author/Illustrator of this work has been asserted by her in accordance
with the Copyright, Designs and Patent Act 1988
This book has been typeset in Adobe Garamond Pro
Printed in the United Kingdom

British Library Cataloguing in Publication Data:
A catalogue record for this book is available from the British Library
ISBN -978-0-9562141-9-5

www.greenbirdbooks.com

LET'S GO
DUA CATCHING

WRITTEN & ILLUSTRATED

ANAYA NAYEER

'Assalaamu Alaikum!' This is Eysah and Mr Cat. They are going dua catching. Would you like to come along?

here

ok

we

go

On Monday, they marched through a great green land, singing, 'Allahu Akbar, we're going on a journey to catch my dua. Just wait and see!'

On Tuesday, they sailed over a sea, singing, 'Allahu Akbar, we're going on a journey to catch my dua. Just wait and see!'

On Wednesday, they crossed a hot desert and came across a sleeping Bedouin. So they sang quietly, 'Allahu Akbar, we're going on a journey to catch my dua. Just wait and see!'

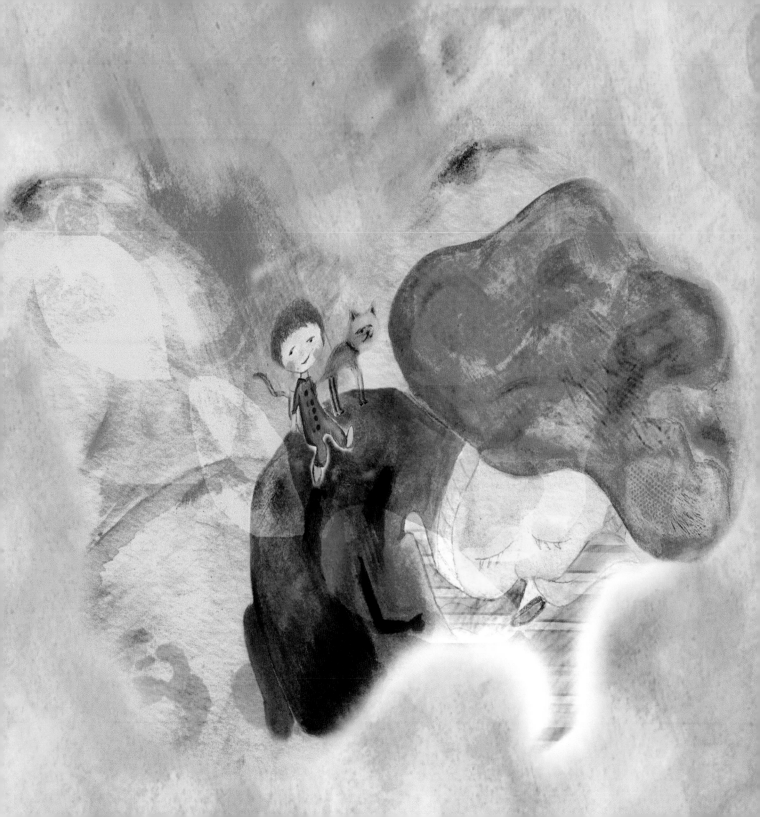

On Thursday, they climbed an enormous white mountain, singing, 'Allahu Akbar, we're going on a journey to catch my dua. Just wait and see!'

On Friday they watched the night sky, singing, 'Allahu Akbar, we're going on a journey to catch my dua. Just wait and see!'

The next day, Eysah was very tired.

So he decided to rest at a beautiful masjid.

When he looked up, he saw an old man
coming towards him.

Eysah said, 'Assalaamu Alaikum, I am looking for my dua. I forgot to pray for my sister, Aisha. I am so sad!'

The old man smiled and said, 'All duas go to Almighty Allah. He is our Creator and knows everything. Why don't you make a new dua for Aisha?'

So Eysah placed his hands together and closed his eyes. He then made dua and it was beautiful. It had Aisha and all of his friends playing around their apple tree at home.

اَلْحَمْدُ لِلَّهِ الَّذِي
أَحْيَانَا بَعْدَ مَا أَمَاتَنَا
وَإِلَيْهِ النُّشُورُ

With that, Eysah woke up. It had all been a dream! Eysah and Aisha decided to make a new dua together.

'Thank you Allah, for everything we have, but best of all for having each other. Ameen!'